EXPLORING HISTORY
CHINA

WANG TAO

Belitha Press
In association with the Royal Geographical Society

Previous page:
Fishermen on the River
Li, Guilin, in southern
China. The Chinese
always say 'the
landscape of Guilin is
the best in the world'.

This page: **A** picture of
the Tiantai Mountains
taken from a Chinese
traveller's diary.

Foreword

Many animals, birds and fish regularly travel over great distances. What sets people apart is the ability to explore and discover. An explorer is someone who is curious about the world and if you are curious enough to read this book then you too have become an explorer.

Exploring is not just about getting into a plane or sailing on a boat to a place you have never been before – you have to record what you see, listen to the people you meet and learn about the place you find. This book follows in the footsteps of all good explorers by discovering the people, history and countryside of the land before it was 'discovered' by outside peoples as well as telling the stories of the adventurers who travelled there for the first time.

Explorers have travelled all over the world and have been helped throughout the centuries by the inhabitants of the lands they visited. People have shown outsiders their homes, helped them carry their loads, paddled their canoes, showed them amazing animals and often housed, clothed, fed, rescued and cured them. This book tells you about these people as well as the explorers they helped or fought with.

Travellers have explored the world for many different reasons. Early adventurers like Marco Polo (1254-1324) and Ibn Battuta (1304-1364) journeyed with trading caravans. Christopher Columbus (1451-1506), Ferdinand Magellan (1480-1521), Captain James Cook (1728-1779) and John Franklin (1786-1847) were sent by governments to investigate the geography of the world. Other explorers were merchants, scientists, colonialists, artists, adventurers, naturalists or even conquerors like Francisco Pizarro (1475-1541) who destroyed the Inca Empire that he discovered.

The Royal Geographical Society is proud to support the *Exploration Into* series of books. Ever since it was founded in 1830, the RGS has helped and inspired famous explorers like Robert Scott (1868-1912) and Dr David Livingstone (1813-1873). Today, the RGS helps modern-day explorers climb the world's mountains, walk across its deserts, cycle through its continents, sail up its rivers, dive deep under the oceans and discover the scientific secrets of nature. We invite you to pick up *Exploration Into* and start your own journey of discovery . . .

DR JOHN HEMMING, *Director and Secretary, Royal Geographical Society, London*

Contents

An old farmer walks with his bamboo basket on his back. The majority of the Chinese population are farmers.

RUSSIA

Hangayn Mountains

Altai Mountains

Ulaan Baatar

Karakoram

MONGOLIA

Gobi Desert

Da Xing'An Mountains

Xiao Xing Mountains

Heilong River

Changbai Mountains

Tian Mountains

Tarim River

Pamir Mountains

Tarim Basin

Takla Makan Desert

Altun Mountains

Qilian Mountains

Inner Mongolian Plateau

Beijing (Peking)

NORTH KOREA

Sea

Bo Hai

Ptongyang

Kunlun Mountains

Lake Qinghai

Yellow River

Seoul

SOUTH KOREA

Yellow Sea

Hindu Kush

Indus River

Bayan Har Mountains

C H I N A

PAKISTAN

Tibetan Plateau

TIBET

Lhasa

New Delhi

Daxue Mountains

Yangtze River

Lake Dongting

Shanghai

Hangzhou

Lake Poyang

East China Sea

HIMALAYAS

NEPAL

BHUTAN

Kathmandu

Hengduan Mountains

Brahmaputra River

Wenzhou

INDIA

Ganges River

BANGLADESH

Mekong River

Nanpan River

Hongshui River

NORTH PACIFIC

Dacca

Taibei

TAIWAN

Calcutta

MYANMAR (BURMA)

Salween River

THAILAND

Red River

Hanoi

Formosa Strait

Hong Kong

Mouth of the Ganges River

I N D O

LAOS

VIETNAM

Gulf of Tongking

Bay of Bengal

C H I N A

Hainan

South China Sea

The name China probably comes from the ancient **Persian** word Cini. In Ancient India, China was called Cina. The Ancient Greeks called China Seres. All of these words are associated in some way with silk (see pages 14-15).

1 Exploring China

The Story of China

Together with **Mesopotamia**, Egypt, Ancient Greece and India, China is one of the oldest civilizations in the world. Ancient China gave many important inventions to the world, such as paper, printing, the compass and gunpowder. There are many things in your life which originally came from China, such as fireworks, chess, kites, umbrellas and **porcelain** (see page 25). China has also borrowed things from other cultures, such as glass and tobacco. This book explores the fascinating history of the Chinese people and China's relationship with the rest of the world.

The People

More than 1.1 billion people live in China and so the Chinese make up roughly one-fifth of the world's population. Although all of these people are Chinese, many also belong to **ethnic** minorities (such as the Uighurs, the Mongolians and the Miao) and have their own languages, traditions and customs. Some live in the border areas of China, such as the Jinuo and Wa peoples of the high mountains of south-west China.

A Huge Country

China is the third largest country in the world and is bigger than the whole of Europe. Because China is so vast it is divided into 22 regions, called provinces, which are controlled by local governments. These local governments report back to central government in the capital city of Beijing (also known as Peking). A single Chinese province is often larger than a single European country.

*F*armers make terraced fields so that they can grow crops on mountainsides.

The Land

If you follow the outline of China on a map you will find that it looks rather like a chicken, with its head in the north-east and tail in the north-west.

The landscape varies dramatically in different parts of China. The Tianshan Mountains and the Gobi Desert are in the north-west. The north-east reaches to Siberia, where the temperature can fall as low as −40°C in winter. This north-eastern route was the traditional way Chinese people travelled to Russia, Mongolia, Korea and overseas to Japan. The south of China is **semi-tropical** and has borders with the countries of mainland South East Asia. The mountains in the south-west of China join up with the Himalayas. The longest rivers in China, the Yangtze and Yellow Rivers, both start in the Kunlun Mountains in the west and flow eastwards to the Pacific Ocean. The coast of China runs along this ocean for 12,000 kilometres, and the major ports on the coast, such as Canton and Shanghai, have been gateways to the Pacific Ocean and the rest of the world for centuries.

The Beginnings of Civilization

This map shows the locations of some of the earliest civilizations in China.

In the nineteenth century, Western historians believed that people travelled to China from Mesopotamia about 5,000 years ago. But **archaeologists** have now found traces of human activity all over China from all periods of time.

Peking Man

In 1929, a young Chinese archaeologist, Pei Wenzhong (1904-82), found a seven-million-year-old human skull which he called 'Peking Man'. Peking Man lived in caves at Zhoukoudian, a hilly area near China's modern-day capital of Beijing. We know that millions of years ago people made stone tools and used fire to cook and to protect themselves from the cold. Seven million years ago Zhoukoudian was surrounded by rivers and **grasslands**, and wild animals lived in the bushes and forests. The early humans hunted deer in the forests and gathered fruit from trees to survive.

Yangshao Villages

About 7,000 years ago there were many farming villages along the Yellow River Valley. The people of these villages used polished stone tools, grew **millet**, wheat and barley and collected fruits from the forest and fish from the rivers. They kept animals such as pigs and dogs and made pottery jars to store their food. They decorated their pottery with beautiful patterns of plants, animals and humans. We know from **excavated** human remains that when a person died he or she was buried in a public cemetery behind the houses of the village. Each village built a large central house for public meetings.

This is an artist's impression of a Yangshao village. These villages were usually ruled by female chiefs. The largest building in the illustration is the village meeting house.

J. G. Anderson

One of the most famous foreign archaeologists to work in China was the Swede, J. G. Anderson (1874-1960). When Anderson was young, he took part in expeditions to the North and South Poles. In 1914, Anderson went to China to work as a **geologist**. Later, he became more interested in archaeology. Anderson discovered the **Neolithic** village of Yangshao in Henan province and worked at Zhoukoudian, where Peking Man was found.

These modern-day rice farmers grow and harvest rice in the same way as their ancestors did thousands of years ago.

Rice-growing in the South

People in North China grew millet while people in South China grew rice. Chinese archaeologists have found a 7,000-year-old settlement at Hemudu near Hangzhou Bay, where wooden houses were built above the ground on stilts. The people of Hemudu were among the earliest rice farmers in the world and some of the objects they made from bone are beautifully carved with images of birds and plants.

The early inhabitants of North and South China are the ancestors of modern-day Chinese people. The people of these two areas had very different life-styles and yet they traded goods with each other and learned about each others' culture. These people made beautiful carvings on stone, jade and bones and painted their pottery with distinctive designs. Together, the early humans of North and South China created the beginnings of Chinese civilization.

This is the reconstructed head of Peking Man. He has high eyebrows and a pointed mouth.

7

This bronze cooking pot is decorated with a human face and animal claws. It dates from the fourteenth to the eleventh centuries BCE.

A thirteenth-century BCE bronze taotie.

This Shang bronze was used to hold food during religious ceremonies.

Bronze-Age China

The Bronze Age began in China in about 3000 BCE. It differed from the European Bronze Age because the Chinese did not make many bronze farming tools. They concentrated on making elaborate bronze objects for use in their religious ceremonies.

In about 1600 BCE the Shang established their rule (called a **dynasty**) in the Central Plains (see map). The Shang moved their capital city many times and finally settled at Anyang, in Henan province. They built palaces, royal tombs and workshops for making bronze weapons and other objects. Many Shang **bronzes** have a distinctive two-eyed mask design called a *taotie*.

The Shang had many **colonies** and were frequently at war. In the middle of the eleventh century BCE, the Shang Dynasty was defeated by the Zhou from north-west China.

The green area shows where ancient bronze objects have been found.

The Rise of the Zhou

When the Zhou overthrew the Shang, the Zhou king divided up the land and gave it to his close family and relatives. He gave them all the title of 'lord' and gifts such as chariots, **textiles** and slaves. Details of these gifts were often written on bronzes which were passed down from generation to generation.

The Zhou kings lived in their capital and travelled out to the country to worship the mountains and rivers in different seasons. At the beginning of the Zhou's reign more than 70 states were given to members of the royal family to rule. These people later fought each other for land and power. In 841 BCE, King Li was thrown out of his palace by his own people and they governed the country for the next 14 years. There was constant conflict between the Zhou and many minority peoples (whom the Zhou called Barbarians). The next king, Ping, had to move his capital to Luoyang in 770 BCE because **nomads** from the west invaded the old capital, Gaojing.

The Shang and Zhou people liked hunting rabbits, birds, tigers and rhinoceros.

The Earliest Chinese Writing

Early Chinese writing has been found carved into bones at Anyang. Although there are some earlier **inscriptions** on Neolithic pottery, these bones show the earliest surviving example of the written Chinese language. Some of the words (called characters) carved into ox bones and turtle shells refer to religion (and so are called oracle bones) and some of them are historical records. If the Shang king wanted to know what the weather was going to be like his advisers made cracks on a prepared animal bone, or sometimes several bones, using a heated rod. Then they read the cracks: *Tomorrow is a fine day, no rain. Tomorrow is not a fine day, it will rain.* The information was written on the bones and put away for future reference.

These Shang oracle bones (fourteenth century BCE) record a family history (above and below).

Early Philosophers

The Zhou Dynasty survived longer than any other dynasty in Chinese history (c.1100-221 BCE). But the last 300 years of the dynasty's reign were very violent and are called the Warring States Period. From the seventh century BCE onwards, China was in a constant state of unrest. The Zhou kings lost control of the country and semi-independent lords and dukes fought each other to gain more land. Early Chinese **scholars** reacted to this situation by creating new ways of thinking about the world, called philosophy. New theories of philosophy and hundreds of different philosophical schools flourished.

The Philosophy of Confucius

Confucius (551-479 BCE) was born into a family of **officials** in the state of Lu, in the modern-day province of Shandong. He admired earlier wise men and felt sad about the lost 'paradise' of previous Chinese societies. He tried to restore old customs and ceremonies through his teachings. His pupils recorded his teachings which later became the state religion of the Chinese government and were followed by every Chinese official.

This eighteenth-century drawing by a Japanese artist is based on the legend that Confucius was once Laozi's student.

Confucius' Rivals

Laozi (c.604-531 BCE) was the founder of the Daoist (or Taoist) religion. Laozi thought that non-action is the best solution to any problem and that returning to nature is the Right Way to Live, or the *Dao* of things. Legend says that Laozi was travelling on an ox-cart and a gatekeeper stopped him and persuaded him to write down his philosophy. Laozi's book has been translated into many languages.

Mozi (c.479-381 BCE) was Confucius' main rival. Unlike Confucius, Mozi opposed music and lavish ceremonies, such as elaborate burials. He hated war and believed in 'love-all' – loving everyone regardless of their social status, age or sex. Mozi had many students and all their writings were published under his name. Mozi and his followers were very interested in science and probably made the first kites.

This is the Daoist Symbol of the Cosmos. It represents a symbolic balance between the Yin (dark section) and Yang (light section) aspects of the world.

A later philosopher, Zhuang Zhou (c.369-290 BCE), refused to take any official government posts, preferring to live in poverty. He believed that people should respect nature and once dreamt he had become a butterfly. He then asked his students if they thought he was Zhuang Zhou dreaming he was a butterfly, or whether he was a butterfly dreaming he was Zhuang Zhou.

2 The Great Empire

The First Emperor

The Warring States Period ended in 221 BCE, when the Qin state in the north-west of China managed to unite the whole country. The king of Qin then became the First Emperor – Shihuangdi (259-210 BCE) – of China, reigning from 221-210 BCE.

A map of the Qin Empire at its height.

A portrait (below) of the First Emperor, Qin Shihuangdi. The picture (left) illustrates Qin's soldiers burying scholars and burning their books. We can tell that this is a later drawing because books of Qin's time were written on bamboo slips, not on paper (as in the picture).

To strengthen his rule, Qin Shihuangdi ordered that all works of literature and philosophy were to be burned and 500 scholars buried alive. He built lavish palaces, put up stone tablets that praised his achievements and travelled all over China. Qin Shihuangdi believed that it was possible to live forever. He sent hundreds of young boys and girls into the sea to search for the magic plant of long life. But they all drowned and Qin Shihuangdi only lived for 49 years. He died while touring China and his death was kept secret for weeks, until the smell of his body was overpowering. Just four years after Qin Shihuangdi's death, the Qin Dynasty was overthrown by a peasant uprising in 206 BCE.

The Terracotta Army

In 1974, a peasant digging for water accidentally discovered an army made of **terracotta** a few miles away from the First Emperor of Qin's tomb. Thousands of clay soldiers, horses and chariots have now been excavated. They are all life-sized and have different faces, hairstyles and expressions. Several pits containing clay soldiers surround the emperor's tomb because he believed that his terracotta army would protect his soul in the **afterlife**.

The four pits that surround the emperor's tomb contain the terracotta army – one pit alone contains 6,000 figures.

Qin Shihuangdi's Tomb

As soon as he became emperor, Qin Shihuangdi started to build his own tomb at Li Mountain, near modern-day Xi'an. It took seven million workers ten years to finish. The burial chamber floor was made of copper and the tomb contained a model of the royal palace with its numerous **treasuries** and precious objects.

The Han Dynasty

Liu Ban (256-195 BCE), a low-ranking official of the Qin government, defeated all his enemies during the peasant uprising and established the Han Dynasty in 202 BCE.

During the Han Dynasty, agriculture developed rapidly and ox ploughs and iron tools were widely used. China became very rich and powerful. The Han emperors expanded their territory in all directions.

A portrait of the Han emperor Liu Ban.

This map shows the extent of the Han Empire at its height.

The Yellow Turban Rebellions

In the third century CE, many popular Daoist sects (groups) rose up against the Han government and brought about its collapse. People belonging to the sects often wore yellow turbans around their heads, so their uprisings have been called the Yellow Turban Rebellions. China sank into a new period of unrest after these rebellions. Between 304-580 CE, there were power struggles on the Central Plains, and on the northern and western frontiers many minority peoples established their own kingdoms.

This picture shows two craftsmen chopping and soaking bamboo for making paper.

The Invention of Paper

Paper was invented in China in the second century BCE. People started to use plants, such as hemp, to make thin paper. Before this time, people wrote on pottery, bones, stone, silk, wood and bamboo. In 105 CE Cai Lun, an official of the Han court, improved the technology of paper-making and his name has been associated with paper-making ever since. Eight centuries later, papermaking spread to the Arab world and from there to Europe.

The Great Wall was not built entirely by the First Emperor, some of it existed before him, but he did make it much longer.

The Silk Road and the Romans

A map of the Silk Routes. The illustration (bottom) shows a camel caravan travelling across the desert.

This eighth or ninth-century painted silk was discovered along the ancient Silk Road.

In the first century CE, the Roman Empire was at the height of its power. It became fashionable in Rome to make clothes out of soft, transparent (see-through) silk from China. The price of silk was very high in Rome: the best Chinese bark (a particular kind of silk) cost as much as three hundred denarii (a Roman soldier's salary for an entire year). Silk was brought to Rome in many different ways, usually by land. The most popular route crossed the Gobi Desert, Bactria, and Seleucia before finally reaching Rome. This route was called the Silk Road. Often the silk passed through the hands of many traders on its way to Rome. The Chinese also developed a taste for foreign imports, such as glass, precious stones, perfume, linen, coral and pearls which all came from Rome and Egypt.

A *modern traveller walks along the ancient Silk Road to Karakoram.*

The First Chinese Traveller to Central Asia

In 138 BCE the Han emperor, Wudi (156-87 BCE), sent his official Zhang Qian (died 114 BCE) to seek **allies** to fight the **Huns** of the north-west grasslands. But the Huns captured Zhang Qian and imprisoned him for ten years. Zhang Qian managed to escape and return to the capital, Chang'an. In 119 BCE, Zhang Qian made his second trip to Central Asia, this time with a team of 300 people. Zhang Qian brought back lots of information about Central Asia and visitors from the Wusun tribe.

The people of Central Asia and China had been trading with each other long before Zhang Qian's mission, but Zhang Qian was the first person to record anything about Central Asia and its people. As a result of his mission, the Silk Road became even busier than before. Chinese silk and cast-iron objects were **exported** to the West, and grapes, walnuts and **pomegranates** were brought into China.

The Rediscovery of the Silk Road

The Silk Road was buried for more than a thousand years. During the late nineteenth century European explorers began searching for the lost cities and cultures of the Silk Road. The most famous of these explorers were Sven Hedin (1865-1952) and Aurel Stein (1862-1943) (see box).

Sven Hedin and Aurel Stein

The Swedish explorer Sven Hedin made four expeditions to China. In 1893 he crossed the Pamir Mountains and reached Kashgar, temporarily losing his sight because of the extreme cold and **mountain sickness**. During his second expedition in 1899, Hedin discovered the long-lost city of Loulan in the Takla Makan Desert. In 1906 Hedin travelled to Tibet and the Himalayas to study archaeology, the climate and plant life. Hedin's last expedition, in 1927, was with many Chinese scholars to Inner Mongolia, Ningxia, Gansu and Xinjiang, where they made many important archaeological discoveries.

Aurel Stein was a Hungarian-British archaeologist who made three important expeditions from India into China from 1900-1918. He mapped China and carried out archaeological surveys and excavations. During his second expedition Stein met Wang Yuanlu, a Chinese Daoist priest who showed him a fabulous library dating from the fourth to the tenth centuries, which was hidden in the Caves of a Thousand Buddhas at Dunhuang.

Many beautiful images have survived from the eighth and ninth centuries from the Caves of a Thousand Buddhas at Dunhuang.

The Arrival of Buddhism

This giant statue of Buddha is 70 metres high. It was carved out of the side of a mountain in Sichuan during the eighth century.

From India to China

Buddhism was brought to China from India during the first century CE. This religion was founded by Siddharta Gautama, a prince born in about 560 BCE. Siddharta lived in great luxury, but was unhappy with his life. When he was 29, Siddharta gave up his wealth and left his father's palace to travel around India. He spent the remaining 44 years of his life searching for truth on his journey and preached that the best way to find the truth was to **meditate**, be non-violent and moderate in all things. The aim of the Buddhist religion is for an individual to reach a state of personal enlightenment by following Buddha's teachings. Enlightenment is the name given to the state of mind someone reaches when they feel that they can see the true nature of all things.

A Popular Religion

Buddhism was very popular in China from the first to the eighth centuries CE. In 68 CE, the Han emperor, Mingdi, sent his official, Cai Yin, to Central Asia to learn more about Buddhism after a vision of a golden figure appeared to him in a dream. The next morning he asked his ministers what the dream meant and was told that he had seen the Buddha – the god of the west. Cai Yin returned to Luoyang, the new Han capital, with images of the Buddha, Buddhist scriptures and two Buddhist monks. They arrived in Luoyang riding on white horses and the temple built for them was named the White Horse Temple.

Buddhists have carved and painted many images of Buddha. This is the famous seventh-century Longmen Cave near Luoyang.

During the sixth century, the emperor Xiao Yan (464-549) became a Buddhist monk and left his palace on three occasions to seek enlightenment. The government he left behind had to give large sums of money to Buddhist temples in order to persuade Xiao Yan to return.

This is a map of the canals built during the Sui Dynasty.

The Grand Canal

The Grand Canal was an ambitious project started during the Sui Dynasty (seventh century) (see page 18). More than a million people built the canal so that the transportation of rice and weapons between north and south China would be easier. The canal is a thousand kilometres long and was the largest of its type until the eighteenth century when Europeans began to build commercial waterways on a similar scale.

Emperor Yang Di built the Grand Canal. He is shown here travelling on the canal followed by a large number of women and servants.

3 The Golden Age

The Centre of the World

An artist's impression of a market scene in the city of Chang'an.

Chang'an

The Tang capital city, Chang'an, was designed by Yu Wenkai and the building work started in 582. It remained the capital throughout the Sui and Tang dynasties. It was designed to be roughly square-shaped, with straight roads running north, south, east and west, dividing the city into different areas. The biggest street was 410 metres wide! There were also royal gardens and a **polo** ground. There was an eastern market where more than 200 different types of Chinese businesses thrived, and a western market for foreign traders and craftworkers, such as silversmiths.

After the fall of the Han Empire, China was split up into many small kingdoms. In 581 General Yang Jian (541-604) set up the Sui Dynasty (581-618) and reunited China by defeating his opponents. In 618 another general of the Sui Court, Li Yan (566-635), joined a rebellion to overthrow the Sui ruler and established the Tang Dynasty (618-906). The Tang Dynasty ruled during the Golden Age of Chinese history. During the next 100 years of stability, agriculture and the textile industry advanced rapidly and the population of China increased. The granary in Luoyang could store 360 million kilogrammes of grain – about half the total grain reserves of the state. The arts flourished and poetry in particular became popular throughout the country. Today we know of more than 10,000 poets from this period.

This picture illustrates the Tang emperor, Xuanzong, watching his favourite concubine, Yang Guifei, trying to get on a horse.

This is a map of the Tang Empire showing Chang'an at its centre.

The Capital City

During the Tang Dynasty, the capital Chang'an was one of the largest cities in the world. Merchants came from all over the world to buy and sell goods. There was also an early banking system that allowed traders to deposit, and sometimes borrow, money. Chang'an was a truly international city with Korean, Japanese, Burmese, Arab, Persian and African residents. These people were not only traders, but also scholars, monks, musicians, dancers and athletes. Many aspects of foreign life became popular in Chang'an, such as the Persian game of polo, which was played by Tang aristocrats. The Tang emperor Xuanzong (685-762) even held international polo matches in his pleasure gardens and was a member of the Chinese polo team.

Princess Wencheng's Marriage

Chinese emperors usually tried to marry their daughters into the royal families of neighbouring states. Their aim was to maintain good relations with their neighbours and so protect the borders of their land. In 640, Songzan Ganbu (617-50), the King of Tibet, made a marriage proposal to the emperor of China's daughter, the Princess Wencheng. A year later the princess married the king. When Wencheng went to Tibet she took some of the most up-to-date Chinese agricultural and weaving methods, some craftworkers and the Chinese calendar. Songzan Ganbu built a castle and a palace for Wencheng and she lived in luxury in Lhasa, the capital.

The First Empress

Wu Zetian was born in 624. Her father was a merchant who later became an official, but he died when she was only nine years old. At the age of 14 she was selected to be an **Imperial concubine** and later she became the wife of Emperor Gaozong. In 690 he died and she became the first empress in Chinese history. During her reign she changed the examination system for selecting officials for central and local government so that people from poor backgrounds would have a chance to become officials. The Empress Wu was a Buddhist and built many temples and **pagodas**. Wu Zetian died in 705.

The First Empress, Wu Zetian.

19

Travelling Monks and Famous Poetry

After 17 years, Xuanzang returned to the Tang capital, Chang'an, from India. He was welcomed by the emperor and people lined the road to catch a glimpse of him. His boxes of Buddhist books followed behind him on horses.

The journey from China to India was long and difficult. This ninth-century drawing shows a travelling monk with all his luggage on the road to India.

From the fourth to the eighth centuries, Buddhism became more popular than ever and many Buddhist monks longed to go to India to visit the birthplace of the Buddha.

Travelling Monks

The first recorded pilgrimage to India was made by the monk Faxian (sometimes called Fa Hsien), who left Chang'an in 399. When he arrived at Khotan, near the Chinese border, Faxian was impressed by the popularity of Buddhism there. He crossed the Pamir Mountains and visited many temples and shrines in Afghanistan and northern India. Twelve years later he returned home by sea.

Another travelling monk was Xuanzang (602-64). In some ways, Xuanzang's journey was even more difficult than Faxian's because the early Tang emperors did not allow people to travel abroad. Despite this, Xuanzang left Chang'an in 627 to travel to India. After travelling through Xinjiang, Afghanistan, Pakistan, India, Bangladesh and Sri Lanka, he returned to Chang'an in 645 with hundreds of volumes of Buddhist texts written in **Sanskrit**. The Tang emperor Taizong offered him financial support so that the Buddhist books could be translated into Chinese.

Many Buddhist books have been translated into Chinese. This is part of the ninth-century Lotus Sutra *which was brought to London by Aurel Stein, from Dunhuang.*

Famous Poetry

During the Tang period every educated person could write both poetry and prose. Poetry even became an important part of the examination to get a job in local government! The most famous Tang poets are Li Bo (701-62) and Du Fu (712-70), whose poems are still popular in China today.

Li Bo

Li Bo was born in Chinese Central Asia in 701. As a young man he travelled a great deal and wrote poems wherever he went. Li Bo was so famous that Emperor Xuanzong invited him to join the court at Chang'an, but Li Bo did not get on well with the officials there and left. It is said that he drowned in a river trying to catch the reflection of the moon in the water.

Li *Bo*

Du Fu

Du Fu is famous as a poet of Chinese history. He was born into an official's family and passed the examinations to become an official himself. Du Fu was a good friend of Li Bo's and they travelled together through Henan and Shandong. While Li Bo's poems are very playful and entertaining, Du Fu's poems reflect the more serious side of life and society.

Du *Fu*

Two Poems

The first poem is by Li Bo and the second by Du Fu.

My native country, untroubled times are always in my thoughts.
My friend is lodging in the Eastern mountains,
Dearly loving the beauty of valleys and hills,
At green spring he lies in the empty woods,
And is still asleep when the sun shines on high.

Well said, Chang'an looks like a chessboard –
Won and lost for a hundred years, sad beyond all telling.
The mansions of princes and nobles all have new lords,
And another generation wears the caps and robes of office.
Due north in the mountain passes the gongs and drums shake.
To the chariots and horses campaigning in the west the winged
  dispatches hasten.
While the fish and dragons fall asleep and the autumn river
  turns cold.

4 China After the Tenth Century

Trade and Cities

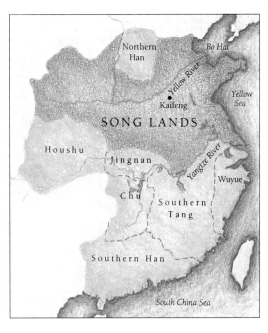

The purple area shows the centre of the Song Dynasty. The orange area shows the states which were brought under Song control.

Another peasant rebellion at the end of the ninth century led to the downfall of the Tang Dynasty and once again China was divided into different kingdoms. In 960 General Zhao Kuangyin (927-76) snatched the throne from the emperor, who was only seven years old. He named his new dynasty the Song Dynasty (960-1279), and made Kaifeng his capital city.

Mining, textiles, papermaking and printing all developed very quickly during the Song Dynasty. The porcelain industry was particularly important. Though porcelain had been exported to Japan, Korea, South Asia and Africa during the Tang Dynasty, improvements in shipping, such as the invention of the compass (see box on page 31), meant that more porcelain could be traded overseas.

An example of Song porcelain.

This famous scroll (rolled) painting measures over five metres when it is unrolled and is called Spring Festival on the River.

A Wealthy City

Kaifeng was blessed with natural advantages. It was surrounded by a natural moat and trade flourished in the city because of its position in the middle of China. There were hundreds of 24-hour restaurants, and many markets and theatres to entertain the thousands of merchants passing through. All types of theatre were popular and performances of opera, puppetry and acrobatics were held in massive theatres – the largest theatre could hold more than 1,000 people. Festivals were held every week in the famous Xiangguo Temple, where people came to buy and sell clothes, books, furniture and pets.

Paper Money

The Chinese invented paper money during the Song period. Paper money had two main advantages over money made out of silver, gold, copper or iron: it was easier to carry around and the copper and iron could be saved for use in everyday objects. Names and **seals** were printed and written on paper money by the government officials who issued them. When Marco Polo (see pages 28-9) travelled to China in the thirteenth century he was so impressed by paper money that he described how it was made, used and valued. Paper money was not used in Europe until the seventeenth century.

A square was cut in the middle of Chinese coins so that merchants could carry them around on strings. The 'coins' above are actually money charms.

Silver was one of the important currencies in China. This picture shows a silversmith cutting ingots (blocks).

The lion dance is performed during the Chinese new year celebrations. It is usually performed by two or three people.

The Arts and Sciences

Scholars and artists were highly respected at the Song court. In this picture Emperor Huizong is entertaining his guests.

Most Chinese books were printed with this type of wood-block.

Many outstanding scientific discoveries were made during the Song period. Sheng Kuo (1031-95) wrote a famous book, *Dream Stream Essays,* which explored **astronomy**, chemistry, mathematics, geology, **physics**, architecture and medicine. This book tells us about many inventors and their creations.

Printing

Before printing was invented, every book had to be copied by hand. In the seventh century, the Chinese invented wood-block printing. The text was first written on a piece of thin paper, then glued face down on to a wooden plate. The characters (letters or words) were carved out to make a wood-block printing plate, which was used to print the text. Wood-block printing took a long time as a new block had to be carved for every page in a book.

Bi Sheng (died c.1051) invented movable type printing from 1041-8. He made a separate block for each character out of clay, so that they could be arranged into a block for printing, and then later reused. This invention was as revolutionary in its time as the computer has been in the twentieth century. Books could be printed more easily and faster than ever before. For example, in 1298, 100 copies of a 60,000-word book were printed in less than a month.

Calligraphy and Painting

During the Song period, officials and rich merchants enjoyed all the arts, but especially **calligraphy** and painting. The Song emperor, Huizong (1082-1135), was an artist and kept a painting school at his court. Artists who passed the school's exams could become professional painters.

Porcelain

The Song period was the Classical Age of the porcelain industry. Song porcelain is renowned for its beauty and also for the way it was made. For example, the Longquan kiln in Zhejiang province could fire (bake) 20,000-25,000 pots at once. In the eleventh century, the art of porcelain-making found its way to Central Asia. Europeans didn't start to make porcelain until the fifteenth century.

Gunpowder

Gunpowder is a mixture of **saltpetre**, **sulphur** and charcoal. In the tenth century, weapon-makers in China discovered that if they combined gunpowder and arrows they could create a new weapon. This new explosive crossbow destroyed their enemies. Forty thousand workers produced several thousand of these weapons every day in the Song capital. In the middle of the thirteenth century, the Arabs learned how to make gunpowder from the Chinese and called it 'China snow'. Europeans eventually found out about gunpowder from the Arabs.

This picture shows two Chinese soldiers using crossbows.

Medicine

Chinese doctors use herbal medicine and acupuncture to cure their patients. When they treat patients with acupuncture they place needles at various points on the body to cure illness: for example, needles in the hand sometimes help to relieve headaches.

In 1026, Wang Weiyi, a doctor in the royal hospital, designed two bronze statuettes showing all the acupuncture needle points on the human body. This type of model is still used for teaching medical students today.

Li Shizhen (1518-93) wrote his magnificent book, *Compendium of Materia Medica*, in the sixteenth century. It illustrates nearly 2,000 herbs and lists 11,000 remedies.

Astronomy

As early as the second century CE, Zhang Heng (78-139 CE) built a **celestial globe**. In 1088, Han Gonglian designed the first water-driven astronomical clock in the world. It took three years to build, was 12 metres tall and had nearly 200 wooden puppets in its five levels which beat drums and made beautiful sounds.

The science of astronomy was very advanced in China. This is an eighteenth-century drawing of the royal observatory.

5 New Travellers

The Mongols and the Arrival of Foreigners

An *illustrated manuscript showing the fierceness of the Mongol cavalry.*

The Mongols were a tribe of nomads who lived on the Mongolian grasslands, or steppes. In the thirteenth century Genghis Khan (c.1167-1227) united all the nomads of the steppes (about six large tribes) by defeating them all in battle, and in doing so established the Mongol Empire. When Genghis Khan died, his grandson Kublai Khan (1260-94) led the Mongolian army into battle against the Song Dynasty and defeated it. In 1271, he moved his government to Peking (called Yanjing at the time) and established the Yuan Dynasty. During the thirteenth century, the Mongols took control of large areas of China and Central Asia and even attacked Europe.

The Mongols had various contacts outside China, in particular with the **Muslims** from Central and Western Asia, and they employed many foreigners in their government. More Europeans began to find their way to China and these explorers brought many Chinese inventions back to the West.

There are plenty of stories about the Europeans who travelled to, or wanted to travel to, China during this time. Friar William's expedition was unsuccessful but Marco Polo's journey (see pages 28-29) was a success.

Yuan Drama

The Mongols took great pleasure in drama. As it was difficult for Chinese people to get an official post in the Mongolian government, many Chinese writers devoted their time and talents to writing plays for the theatre instead. Guan Hanqing (c.1220-1300) was the most famous playwright of this time. He wrote more than 60 plays and some of them are still enjoyed by people today. Ji Junxiang was another Yuan playwright. His work, *Chinese Orphan*, was performed in Paris in August, 1755.

In *this scene from a Yuan play, the girl is playing a musical instrument called a* piba.

A *Mongol woman and her children in front of their yurt home (above). The grasslands of Mongolia (below and background) are home to 20,000,000 people.*

Friar William

Friar William was a priest at the court of the French king Louis IX. In 1253 he decided to travel to the East to bring Christianity to the Mongols. He set off from Constantinople (modern-day Istanbul in Turkey) and made his way towards the Black Sea (see map). After travelling for a month by boat and on horseback he met the Mongols and stayed with them for several months before finally reaching Karakoram. The Mongols thought that Friar William was a spy and wouldn't let him travel freely. Friar William wrote about the people he met and the places he visited. He described Mongolian yurts, or houses: *'They set up the dwelling in which they sleep on a circular frame of interlaced sticks converging into a little round hoop on the top.'* Unfortunately, Friar William never crossed the Great Wall and did not reach China, but he probably met some Chinese people because he mentioned the Song Dynasty (see pages 22-3), Chinese paper money and Chinese writing.

The Story of Marco Polo

Marco Polo (1254-1324) was born in Venice. Marco's father, Nicolas, and uncle, Maffeo, were merchants who travelled to Central Asia to do business in 1260. At Bokhara they met some Chinese **envoys** who invited them to China. They arrived in China in 1265, stayed for about a year, and met Kublai Khan. They returned to Venice in 1269, but left again for China in 1271. This time Marco went with them and didn't return to Venice until 1295, 24 years after he had set out on his adventure.

A Difficult Journey

The Polos journeyed towards the Persian Gulf, passed through the city of Baghdad and sailed up the Tigris River before walking across western Turkestan, through Balkh, and the Pamir Mountains. Their journey was very dangerous as they had to overcome all the difficulties of crossing high, cold mountains and hot, waterless deserts. Finally, four years after they had left Venice, they met Kublai Khan at Shangtu, the Mongolian capital. Marco Polo stayed in China for 17 years, travelling all over the country and writing about everything he saw and did.

Marco Polo in Peking

Marco was impressed by the city of Peking (modern-day Beijing). He described the palace, streets and markets where he saw paper money for the first time. The walled city had 12 gates, which was more than any European city of the time. The streets were very wide and ran straight across the city. Merchants brought precious stones, pearls, spices and many more things from all over the world to sell in the markets.

A picture of Marco Polo and his father and uncle from a Spanish map.

Markets and Banquets

In his famous book, *The Travels of Marco Polo,* Marco wrote about the markets of Peking: *'No fewer than a thousand packhorses and carriages, loaded with raw silk from the Chinese provinces, make their daily entry'.* He also described banquets held in the royal palace. The banqueting hall was large enough to seat 6,000 guests and the tables were decorated with carved animals and bowls and cups of silver and gold. At important banquets an orchestra played, singers and dancers performed and elephants and lions were put on show.

Marco Polo and his father and uncle leaving Venice for China.

Marco Polo also visited Suzhou which is near Hangzhou.

Marco Polo in Hangzhou

Kublai Khan, appointed Marco Polo as an official of the **Privy Council** in 1277 and for three years he was a tax inspector in Yangzhou. He frequently visited Hangzhou, another city very near Yangzhou. At one time Hangzhou was the capital of the Song Dynasty (see pages 22-3) and had a beautiful lake and many canals, rather like Marco's home town of Venice. Marco fell in love with it and wrote: *'There are said to be 12,000 bridges, mostly of stone, though some are of wood. Those over the main channels and the chief thoroughfare are built with lofty arches and are so well designed that big ships without a mast can pass under them, and yet carts and horses also pass over them, so well is the street level adjusted to the height.'*

This map shows the journeys of Marco Polo. Marco, his father and his uncle travelled to many places before they reached China.

Ibn Battuta

Ibn Battuta (1304-68) was a great Arab traveller who visited China in the fourteenth century. Arab and Iranian traders were the main contacts between China and Europe during the fourteenth century and sea trading developed rapidly. Muslims went to South East Asia and China to do business and a number of them lived in cities on the south-east coast of China, particularly in Quanzhou and Guangzhou (modern-day Canton).

Ibn Battuta was born into a judge's family in Morocco and started his long journey through Africa and Asia when he was only 21. In India Ibn Battuta met some Chinese ambassadors and decided to go to China with them. In April 1346 they set sail from Samudra and reached the coast of China about four months later, after passing through the Maldive Islands, Sri Lanka and Java. Ibn Battuta announced to Chinese officials that he was the ambassador of the Muslim ruler of India and the Chinese emperor invited him to the capital. On his way to Peking (modern-day Beijing) he visited the city of Hangzhou and was welcomed with banquets, plays and canal trips. Like Marco Polo, Ibn Battuta was impressed by Chinese paper money which was still unknown in the West.

Marco Polo's Routes
— 1271-75
--- 1275-95

Zheng He's Journeys

In the middle of the fourteenth century the Chinese people overthrew the Mongol Yuan Dynasty, and restored their own rule in China. This period became known as the Ming Dynasty (1368-1644). The new emperor was Zhu Yuanzhang. He was also known as the beggar king, because he had spent some years as a travelling monk before his successful rebellion against the Mongols. The new Ming capital was Peking and it took 13 years to build the royal palace.

During the Ming Dynasty, China's relations with other countries underwent a number of changes. In the north, great attention was paid to rebuilding the Great Wall to keep out the nomad invaders of the steppes. The Ming emperors did not allow ordinary people to travel to foreign lands, but they did let their officials travel abroad in order to increase their political influence, particularly in South East Asia.

Zheng He's story was described in seventeenth-century popular fiction. This picture is taken from one of these popular books. The soldier is holding a banner which calls Zheng He 'The Great Commander of the Ming'.

An artist's impression of ships from Zheng He's fleet.

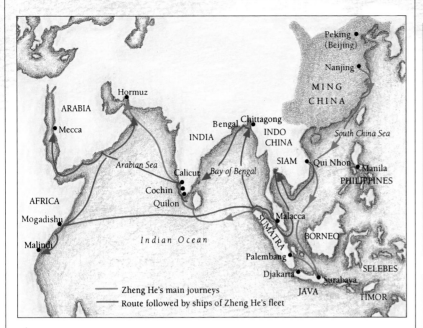

A map of two of Zheng He's expeditions. The purple area shows the Ming Empire.

Zheng He's Treasure Ships

Zheng He (1371-1435) is the most famous sea traveller of Chinese history. He came from a Muslim family in Yunnan and was sent to the royal household to be a **eunuch** and serve the emperor when he was a child. At the imperial court, he became a Buddhist and is known as the Grand Buddhist Eunuch.

Between 1405-33, the emperor Cheng Zu sent Zheng He on seven voyages of discovery overseas, reaching as far as South East Asia, India, the Persian Gulf and East Africa. Zheng He's treasure ships carried enormous quantities of gifts from the emperor, which he presented everywhere he went. On one of his expeditions his 62 ships carried a total of 28,000 men. Each ship weighed 15,000 tonnes. It was the largest fleet in the world at that time.

Shipbuilding

Chinese shipbuilding started in the seventh century BCE and was the most advanced in the world by the thirteenth and fourteenth centuries CE. The most famous Chinese ship was called the sand ship. It had a flat bottom which could take loads of 500-800 tonnes. Chinese shipyards made thousands of ships every year, and these were used by Arab, Asian and African traders as well as the Chinese.

An illustration of one of the earliest compasses. The lodestone (a magnetic iron stone which always points north) floats in water in the centre of the bronze compass.

The Compass

Without a compass, Zheng He's journeys across the Pacific Ocean would not have been possible. The compass was invented in China more than 2,000 years ago. The compass was taken to the Middle East and then to Europe in the twelfth century. It was used in all voyages of exploration. Columbus' discovery of the Americas (1492) and Magellan's round-the-world voyage (1519-21) relied on the compass.

Xu Xiake: An Unusual Traveller

Xu Xiake (1586-1641) was one of the greatest Chinese travellers and explorers. He was born in Jiangyin in the province of Jiangsu. When he was very young he became interested in travel and geography, but because he took care of his old mother he could not go away for long periods of time.

A *portrait of Xu Xiake. His book is still read by many people today.*

A Dangerous Journey

After Xu Xiake's mother died, he travelled to the remotest areas of South China where no one had gone before. In September 1636, he left Jiangyin and headed to Zhejiang with a fellow monk, Jingwen. Unfortunately, Jingwen was murdered by some bandits and Xu carried his ashes to the famous Chicken Feet Mountain in Yunnan and buried him in sacred Buddhist land. Xu continued his journey, but the roads were very difficult to travel along and sometimes there wasn't a road at all. Xu travelled through the provinces of Jiangxi, Hunan, Guangxi and Guizhou, and reached Tengchong in Yunnan in April 1639. After narrowly escaping a fall from the top of a cliff on his way into the city, Xu discovered that he had lost all his money and had to sell his clothes to buy food.

Flowers and Butterflies

Xu Xiake wrote about the huge camelias (a type of flower) he saw in Yunnan. Xu wrote about fabulous flowers again when he visited the famous Taihua Temple in the provincial capital of Kunming. In Dali Xu visited the Butterfly Pool, a place where thousands of butterflies come to rest on a tree by a pool. You can still visit these places today as a modern explorer.

Xu wanted to go on to Burma (modern-day Myanmar) but could not find a guide to take him there. On his journey home he fell ill and died a few months later at the age of 56.

The Three White Pagodas in Dali, Yunnan, built during the Tang period. Xu Xiake described this place in his book.

A *painting on silk of a group of travellers making their way through some of the high mountains of China. The painting dates from the Tang Dynasty (see pages 18-22). Xu Xiake would also have travelled through scenery like this on horseback.*

There are many high mountains in Yunnan which Xu Xiake made detailed notes about in his book.

A *mother and daughter from the mountains of Yunnan.*

6 Europe and China

The Conflict Between Two Different Worlds

A map of European trade routes.

In the fifteenth century, the **Turks** took control of the overland silk and spice route between China and the West. The Europeans were furious about this and sent their sailors to find alternative sea routes to the East so that they could trade with a greater number of people through a greater number of routes. At the same time the Roman Catholic Church wanted to increase its influence in the East and so sent **missionaries** to China.

A Jesuit Priest

Matteo Ricci (1552-1609) was born in Macerata in Italy. He studied in the **Jesuit** school in his home town and then went to Rome to study law. In Rome he became interested in the East (also known at this time as the Orient). In 1582, Ricci arrived in Macao as a missionary. Matteo learned Chinese, befriended many high-ranking Chinese officials and converted some of them to Christianity. He was invited by Emperor Wanli to the Forbidden City (see box on page 38) but failed to convert him to Christianity.

Matteo introduced many aspects of European culture such as **cartography** and mathematics to China. When Ricci died he was buried in Peking (modern-day Beijing).

A Tourist at the Great Wall

Johann Grueber (1623-80) was a German Jesuit priest who set out from Venice for China in 1656. After reaching Peking, he stayed in China for three years and worked as a missionary (along with 56 other Jesuits) baptizing Chinese converts to Christianity.

Grueber left Peking in June 1661 with the French Jesuit monk Albert d'Orville and travelled for 60 days before arriving at Xining, a city near the Great Wall of China. Grueber described the distance between two of the gates on the wall as being a walk of 18 days. Grueber was also impressed by the width of the wall, saying that it was so wide that 'six horsemen may run abreast on it without embarrassing each other'.

After leaving Xining, Grueber and d'Orville travelled on to Lhasa in Tibet and were probably the first Europeans to enter the city.

Matteo Ricci is seen here with his Chinese friend Xu Guanqi, a Ming official and is dressed in traditional Chinese clothes.

The Qing Empire

In 1644, the Ming government was overthrown by a series of peasant rebellions. The Manchus of the Mongolian grasslands then defeated the peasant armies and established their own dynasty called the Qing Dynasty (1644-1911). Like the Mongols, the Manchus were very good soldiers and used their skills to expand the Qing Empire.

By the eighteenth century, Britain was the leading **industrial** power in the West and was keen to trade with China. In 1792, Lord George Macartney (1737-1806) took a delegation of 135 people to China to meet the emperor.

They set sail from Portsmouth in September and arrived in China the following year. Macartney took several artists with him and they recorded the things they saw in beautiful watercolours which they took back to Britain. Macartney took Emperor Qianlong presents as tokens of his goodwill but still failed in his mission to open up more British trade with China. One of the reasons for this failure was Macartney's refusal to kneel down at the feet of the emperor, called kowtowing. The kowtow was a traditional way of showing respect to the emperor.

Emperor Qianlong employed a number of foreigners as court artists. This picture was painted by an Italian called Giuseppe Castiglione (1688-1766).

William Alexander, (1767-1816) one of the artists who went to China with Lord Macartney, made this drawing of the Western Gate of Peking.

The First Opium War

In 1839, the First Opium War broke out between China and Britain over the trade in the drug **opium**. The English East India Company sold opium taken from British India to China in order to pay for Chinese imports such as tea, silk and porcelain. People in China gradually became more and more addicted to opium and spent vast sums of money on the drug. The Chinese government became worried as their treasury was being drained. In 1839 the Chinese government seized more than 20,000 chests of Indian opium in protest and burned them in Canton. The British retaliated by sending 4,000 troops to attack major Chinese ports and cities. The British eventually won the war and a treaty was signed in Nanjing in August 1842, which gave them the right to trade in China. The island of Hong Kong was handed over as part of the peace treaty.

The Second Opium War

On 8 October 1856, Chinese officials arrested Chinese sailors belonging to a British ship in Canton harbour. The British were offended by Chinese interference in their business affairs and demanded an apology. The Chinese

The Taiping Rebellion

It was not only Westerners who caused trouble in China. In 1851, Hong Xiuquan (1814-64) led a rebellion from south-west China and set up his own kingdom which he called the Heavenly Kingdom of Great Peace in Nanjing. Hong came from a farming background and was inspired by Christian teachings. He dreamt that he was the younger brother of Jesus Christ and that it was his mission to save China. His revolution lasted for 13 years and affected half of China.

Chinese ships fighting the British navy during the First Opium War. The Chinese lost the Opium War and were forced to open their ports to foreigners.

The Summer Palace was destroyed by British and French troops in 1856.

government refused to apologize and crowds of protesters burned British shops and factories in Canton. This is how another trading war, called the Second Opium War (even though it had nothing to do with opium), began. Anglo-French troops occupied Peking and set fire to the Imperial Summer Palace. The Summer Palace was one of the finest buildings in the world, built in both Chinese and European styles of architecture. It contained many precious treasures and a royal library. Before destroying the Summer Palace, the British and French troops grabbed as much as they could carry away with them. A British soldier wrote: *'You can scarcely imagine the beauty and magnificence of the buildings we burnt. It made one's heart sore to burn them . . . it was wretchedly demoralizing work for an army. Everybody was wild for plunder.'* Now only a few ruins of the palace are left.

By the early nineteenth century there were plenty of foreigners living in China. This European painting shows different flags hung on ships and buildings.

Scientist Explorers

When China opened its doors to foreigners in the nineteenth century, many Western scientists arrived to study the country's animals and plants. In 1803, William Kerr was sent to China by the Royal Gardens at Kew (London) to collect plants from the Far East. Another famous plant collector was Robert Fortune, who studied at the Royal Botanic Gardens in Edinburgh. In 1843 Fortune was appointed by the Royal Horticultural Society at Chiswick in London as their special plant collector in China. Fortune travelled all over China for nine years and found many new plants.

Between 1864-74 the Frenchman, Père Jean Pierre David (1826-1900), made three journeys into China, travelling from Peking to Mongolia, and from Tibet to Sichuan by boat, horse and on foot. Père David was probably the first Westerner to discover the giant panda in March 1869 while travelling between the borders of Tibet and Sichuan. Some local hunters killed a white 'bear' and sent it to him. Père David wrote in his diary, *'Is it possible that it is new to science?'* and sent the skin and skull of the panda back to Paris where it was identified as a species that was new to the West.

The Last Emperor

The Child Emperor

Pu Yi was born in 1906 when the Qing Dynasty was coming to its end. Emperor Guangxu's wife, Ci Xi, imprisoned him and made herself the head of state. Guangxu died in November 1908 and Ci Xi (called the Empress Dowager) chose two-year-old Pu Yi as the new emperor of China. She knew he was too young to rule, which meant that she would have more power. But the empress died just a few months later. When Pu Yi was five years old, China became a republic (a country with an elected government rather than one ruled by a king or queen), but the new government allowed him to carry on living in the Forbidden City. Pu Yi learned to read and write with his servants and practised calligraphy for hours every day. Pu Yi had a British tutor, Reginald Johnston, who visited the palace almost every day from March 1919 until 1922.

Empress Ci Xi and the child emperor Pu Yi.

The Forbidden City

Peking (modern-day Beijing) was the old capital of the Yuan Dynasty (see page 26). In 1421, Emperor Chengzu, of the Ming Dynasty, decided to move his capital to Peking and turned the Forbidden City into the Imperial Palace. The Forbidden City occupies 720,000 square metres, took 15 years to build and is right in the middle of Peking. It has nearly 100,000 rooms and is surrounded by a moat. The city is divided into two sections: one area is made up of large ceremonial halls for conducting official business and the other contains living quarters and gardens. The front entrance of the palace is called the Gate of Heavenly Peace.

Like all Chinese emperors, Pu Yi had many wives. This photo is of Pu Yi and his favourite wife, Wan Rong, in Tianjin, together with their foreign friends.

During the 1930s, the Japanese expanded their empire and marched into China. Pu Yi was persuaded to go to Manchuria (where he originally came from) by the Japanese to act as the emperor during their occupation. Pu Yi's life was controlled by the Japanese. The Russian army arrested him when the Japanese left China after the Second World War (1939-45). After some time in prison the last emperor of China later worked as a gardener in Peking (modern-day Beijing) and died in 1967 at the beginning of the Cultural Revolution (see pages 43-4).

The First Railway in China

The first railway in China was built in Shanghai in 1874 with money raised by British companies. People came from miles around to see trains for the first time. Often a wall of people would stand along the side of the tracks watching the trains. Tickets were very expensive: the price of a first class ticket from Shanghai to Wusong was the same amount as rice for a family for one month. However, the railway was built without a proper licence and the Chinese government had it dismantled.

Shanghai: An Adventurer's Paradise

Seven hundred years ago, Shanghai was a small fishing village. It became larger during the Yuan (see page 26) and Ming (see pages 30-31) Dynasties, but was often under attack from Japanese pirates. In 1832, the first British boat to China arrived at the port of Wusong, but was fired upon by the Chinese army. The peace settlement of the First Opium War made Shanghai one of the five open ports where Westerners were allowed to trade. More and more foreigners went to Shanghai to do business and hundreds of foreign shops, banks, clubs and restaurants sprang up. Most foreign visitors lived in special districts rented from the government.

The port of Shanghai during the 1930s.

7 Modern China

Revolution and Change

This original poster (left, 1926) shows the Nationalist army defeating the warlords' (local leaders) troops.

The New Culture

On 4 May 1919, about 3,000 students organized a demonstration in Peking to protest against the Treaty of Versailles, the peace treaty signed by the allies after the First World War (1914-18). The treaty gave Japan control over north-east China and the students objected to this. This demonstration was important because it marked the beginning of the 'New Culture' – new ways of scientific and political thinking.

On 10 October 1911, a revolution transformed China from an imperial empire into a republic when the **Manchu** Emperor was overthrown. The first president of China was Sun Yat-Sen (1866-1925) who ruled at the head of his **Nationalist** party.

The Nationalists and the Communists

In 1912, a group of Nationalists, led by Sun Yat-Sen, formed their own party called the Kuomintang, or KMT. This was the beginning of the Nationalist Revolution.

In 1921, a group of people in Shanghai were influenced by the writings of **Karl Marx** and set up the Communist party. After the death of Sun Yat-Sen in 1925, General Chiang Kai-Shek took over the leadership of the Nationalists. In Canton in 1926, Chiang Kai-Shek led the Nationalist army, which joined with the Communists to fight the warlords (powerful landowners) in the north and unite the nation. Once the warlords had been defeated, the Nationalists hunted out Communists, threw them out of the party and killed anyone who opposed them. The Communists fled to Jiangxi, hid in the mountains and gradually rebuilt their power. In 1934 the Nationalists forced the Communists to retreat again. To escape attack the Communists began the Long March.

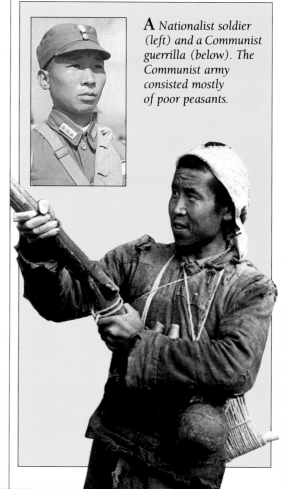

A Nationalist soldier (left) and a Communist guerrilla (below). The Communist army consisted mostly of poor peasants.

The Long March

Late in 1934, the Red Army of about 100,000 people left Jiangxi to travel to Yan'an. They marched through many provinces, climbed over 18 mountain ranges, crossed 24 rivers and trekked through marshes, deserts and snow-covered mountains with only thin cotton clothes to keep them warm. Only one in every five people who set out on the march survived. The people who lived through the march walked 9,600 kilometres in a year. The Communists made Yan'an their headquarters from 1936-45 and conducted **guerrilla** warfare, and educational and agricultural reform programmes from this base.

The leader of the Long March was Mao Zedong (1893-1976), a former teacher who was one of the founding members of the Chinese Communist Party. Mao was the son of a farmer and it was to the country that he returned to find support for his ideas.

Mao liked to give speeches to his soldiers and to ordinary people, but because his accent was so strong people did not find him easy to understand.

Modern China

An American in Yan'an

Edgar Snow (1905-72) was born in Kansas City, USA, and first travelled to China in 1928 as a journalist. Snow became very interested in the Communist Red Army and wrote to his publisher in 1936: *'I am leaving tomorrow for Red China to interview Mao Zedong, and to travel, photograph and write what I please.'* When he arrived in Yan'an, the first Communist leader he met was Zhou Enlai, who later became Prime Minister of China. Snow then met Mao and wrote an account of his visit to Yan'an in his book *Red Star Over China*, which attracted attention all over the world.

Chairman Mao wanted everyone in China to become soldiers so everyone had to do military training.

Chairman Mao Rules China

By 1937 the Nationalist government was losing support because it had failed to stop the Japanese invading China (see page 39). The Communists in Yan'an were fighting the Japanese more successfully through their guerilla tactics and people became aware of this. China was plunged into a civil war between the Nationalists and the Communists in 1946 after the Japanese had been defeated in the Second World War. After nearly three years of fighting, on 1 October 1949, Mao Zedong stood at the Gate of Heavenly Peace in front of the Forbidden City (see page 38) and proclaimed the establishment of the People's Republic of China. The Nationalist government fled to Taiwan, an island off the coast of China in the Pacific Ocean.

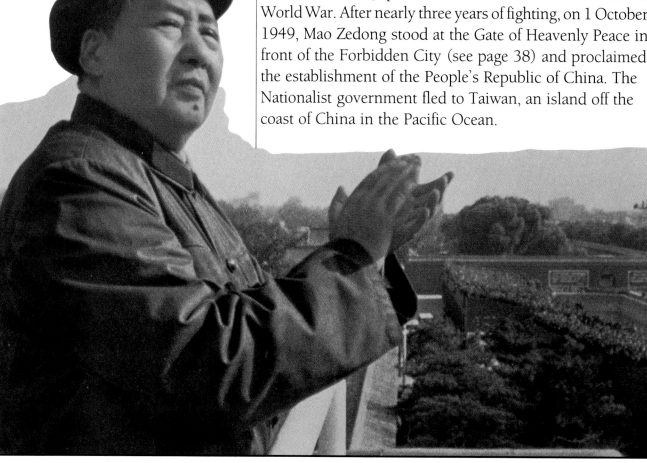
This is a photograph of Chairman Mao addressing a massive crowd of his supporters in Peking in the 1970s.

The Cultural Revolution was a mass demonstration of the people's power. Thousands of people went on marches, holding Chairman Mao's portrait and shouting slogans.

The Cultural Revolution

The Communist government tried to create a new society. In the first years of Communist power many reforms were brought in dividing land equally among the people and forbidding **arranged marriages**. But there were also negative sides to Communist rule. In 1958, Mao announced the Great Leap Forward – a campaign to encourage opponents of the Communists to speak out. With Mao's encouragement, many intellectuals voiced their opinions and were then killed or sent to work in forced labour camps.

In the ten years from 1966 to 1976, Chairman Mao's **Red Guards** tried to destroy traditional customs, books and clothes. This movement was called the Cultural Revolution. It was a disastrous experiment. People who had foreign connections were persecuted and musicians, dancers, surgeons and university professors were exiled to the borders of China where they were forced to do hard labour. Thousands of people died and China's door was firmly shut to the West. When Chairman Mao died on 9 September 1976 at the age of 83, the Cultural Revolution died with him and was re-named the Ten Years of Chaos.

American Zoologists Explore

In 1916, three **zoologists** from the American Museum of Natural History set out with a Chinese interpreter and five Chinese assistants to explore the natural history of Yunnan province. At this time Yunnan was one of the most inaccessible places in China because of its high mountains and ethnic groups who were often at war with each other.

The year-long expedition collected many specimens from the peoples of the province, as an entry from the expedition's diary shows – 'We let it be known that we would pay well for specimens, and there was an almost uninterrupted procession of men and boys carrying long sticks, on which were strung frogs, rats, toads and snakes. They would simply beam with triumph and enthusiasm. Our fame spread and more came, bringing the most ridiculous tame things – pigeons, Maltese cats, dogs, white rabbits, caged birds . . .'

Even children joined the Cultural Revolution. They were called the Little Red Guards.

China Today

China Today

Following the death of Mao Zedong in 1976, China's leaders began repairing the huge damage caused by his 'Cultural Revolution'. The Chinese people were urged to take an interest in overseas countries and the study of foreign languages was strongly encouraged. Trade and investment from outside the country were welcomed. The government relaxed its strict control over the economy with factory and farm owners allowed to set wages and prices. However, these changes in the running of the economy highlighted the differences between richer and poorer regions, and between town and country. Today, corruption among officials is on the increase, 35 million people have lost their jobs as inefficient businesses collapse, and 150 million rural workers are unemployed.

Looking to the Future

China maintains a hard line on territorial claims and human rights. Prosperous Hong Kong and Macao returned to Chinese rights control peacefully in 1997 and 1999. But Tibet is still held down by force and Taiwan is still claimed as a Chinese province, despite US guarantees to defend its independence.

Greater economic freedom to earn bonuses and make profits has not been matched by greater freedom to criticise the government with the Communist party keeping a tight grip on power. In 1989, when student demonstrators occupied Tiananmen Square, in Beijing, to demand greater democracy hundreds were massacred by troops and tanks. The non-violent *Falun Gong* religious movement is banned as a threat to public order.

As the Chinese people grow more prosperous their desire for greater freedom and political power will also increase.

Tiananmen Square

The square in front of the entrance to the Forbidden City, known as the Gate of Heavenly Peace, has always been at the centre of Chinese political life. Ancient imperial governments gave orders in the square and the famous New Culture movement proclaimed itself from the square. After the Communist Revolution, Mao's government pulled down several buildings to make Tiananmen Square the largest of its kind in the world. Mass Communist marches have been held in this huge space and Chairman Mao's body is housed in a building behind it. Tiananmen Square has always been a famous tourist attraction and focus of international attention. On 4 June, 1989, the Square made the headlines once again. Students demonstrating for democracy and reform were massacred by troops in a shocking show of force by the Chinese government.

The student demonstration of 1989 in front of the Forbidden City.

RUSSIA

Siberia

Hangayn Mountains

Altai Mountains

Karakoram

Ulaan Baatar

Xiao Xing'an Mountains

Heilong River

MONGOLIA

Gobi Desert

HEILONGJIANG

• Harbin

XINJIANG

Tian Mountains

Tarim River

Tarim Basin

Takla Makan Desert

Altun Mountains

Inner Mongolian Plateau

NINGXIA HUIZI

NEI MONGOL (INNER MONGOLIA)

• Guyang

Changchun
JILIN

Shenyang •
LIAONING

Changbai Mountains

NORTH KOREA

amir untains

indu Kush

Kunlun Mountains

Qilian Mountains

The Great Wall

Beijing
(Peking) •

Dalian •

Pyongyang •

QINGHAI

Lake Qinghai

Lanzhou •

Taiyuan •

Tianjin

Bo Hai

Sea of Japan

River

C   H   I   N   A

Bayan Har Mountains

GANSU

SHENSI

SHANXI

HEBEI

• Jinan

SHANDONG

Yellow Sea

• Seoul

SOUTH KOREA

AKISTAN

Tibetan Plateau

XIZANG (TIBET)

Daxue Mountains

Xi'an •

Kaifeng •

Yellow River

HENAN

JIANGSU

• New Delhi

• Lhasa

HIMALAYAS

Hengduan Mountains

SICHUAN

Chengdu •

HUBEI

ANHUI

Yangtze River

• Shanghai

Hangzhou •

East China Sea

NEPAL

BHUTAN

Kathmandu •

Brahmaputra River

Lake Dongting

Changsha •

Lake Poyang

Nanchang •

ZHEJIANG

Wenzhou •

NORTH PACIFIC

INDIA

Ganges River

BANGLADESH

Dacca •

Calcutta •

YUNNAN

HUNAN

GUIZHOU

JIANGXI

Nanpan River

Hongshui River

Fuzhou •

FUJIAN

Mouth of the Ganges River

Mekong River

Salween River

Kunming •

GUANGXI ZHUANGZU

GUANGDONG

Guangzhou •
(Canton)

Formosa Strait

Taibei •

TAIWAN

Bay of Bengal

MYANMAR (BURMA)

LAOS

Red River

Hanoi •

Hong Kong •

Macao •

South China Sea

THAILAND

VIETNAM

Gulf of Tongking

A *map of modern-day China. China has three self-governing cities, 22 provinces and five autonomous (self-governing) states.*

China	Europe	Other
c.6000-5000 BCE Farming villages thrive across the Yellow River Valley.	c.6500 BCE Farming begins in Greece and spreads to other areas of Europe.	c.5000 BCE Farming begins in western parts of India.
c.1600-1100 The Shang Dynasty. The Shang make bronzes and write on bones.	c.3000 Use of copper spreads throughout Europe.	c.2500 The horse is domesticated in Central Asia.
c.1040 The Zhou conquer the Shang. c.650 Iron in use.	c.1600 Mycenaean civilization begins in Greece.	c.1200 The Jewish religion emerges. c.1500 The use of iron begins in Turkey.
221 Qin Shihuandgi, the First Emperor. 202 Han Dynasty begins.	510 The Roman Republic is founded.	c.500 The Nok culture in West Africa. c.600-200 The Paracas culture in Peru.
67 CE The Han emperor sends his ministers to India.	43 CE The Roman Empire invades Britain.	30 CE Death of Jesus Christ. Spread of Christianity begins.
584 Emperor Yang Di begins Great Canal. 618-906 The Tang Dynasty rules.	117 The Roman Empire is at its greatest extent.	300s The Ghanaian Empire is founded in West Africa.
627 Xuanzang leaves Chang'an for India. Wood-block printing is invented.	c.542 Bubonic plague spreads through Europe.	622 Mohammed founds the religion of Islam in Arabia.
900-1000 Gunpowder is invented. The compass is used in navigation.	959 The Unification of England.	c.900s Arabs settle the east coast of Africa. 935 The text of the Quran finished.
1272 Marco Polo leaves Venice for China. 1277 Marco Polo meets Kublai Khan.	1066 The Normans conquer England.	c.1000 The Vikings colonize Greenland and travel to America.
1346 Ibn Battuta arrives in China. 1368 The Ming Dynasty rules.	1340s The Bubonic plague continues to spread throughout Europe.	c.1345-1530 The Aztec civilization. 1352 Ibn Battuta travels to Africa.
1405-33 Zheng He makes seven voyages to South East Asia, the Persian Gulf and East Africa.	1492 The first globe is made in Germany by Martin Beheim.	1498 The Portuguese (led by Vasco da Gama) arrive in India.
1514 The first European sailors arrive in China from Portugal.	1532 John Calvin starts the Protestant movement in France.	1530s The European slave trade begins across the Atlantic Ocean.
1582 The Jesuit priest Mattico Ricci arrives in China.	1618 The Thirty Years War of religion starts.	1607 The first English settlement is founded in America (Virginia).
1636 Xu Xiake begins his journey. 1644 The Qing Dynasty rules.	1667 The French begin to expand under Louis XIV.	1680 The Rozvi Empire in Zimbabwe.
1793 Lord Macartney travels to China.	1756 The Seven Years War begins. 1789 The French Revolution begins.	c.1700s European exploration of Africa. 1775-83 The American Revolution.
1839-42 The First Opium War. 1856-60 The Second Opium War.	1807 The slave trade is abolished in Britain.	1789 George Washington becomes the first President of the United States.
1911 The Qing Dynasty ends. China becomes a republic. 1921 Chinese Communist party founded.	1884-85 The West African conference is held in Berlin (Germany).	1857 The Indian Mutiny. 1861 The American Civil Wear begins.
1934 The Long March begins. 1937 Japanese troops invade China.	1914-18 World War I	1915 Africa continues to be divided by foreign powers. 1917 The USA enters World War I.
1949 Chairman Mao establishes the People's Republic of China. 1967 The Cultural Revolution begins.	1939-45 World War II.	1941 The USA enters World War II.
1976 Chairman Mao dies. The Cultural Revolution ends.	1961 The Berlin Wall is built in Germany.	1961 John F. Kennedy becomes President of the USA. 1963 John F. Kennedy is assassinated.
1980s The Chinese government opens its doors to the West for the purposes of trade.	1972 The European Community gains more members.	1965-73 The USA is involved in the Vietnam War.
1989 Pro-democracy demonstrators are killed by the army in Tiananmen Square.	1985 Mikhail Gorbachev becomes the. leader of the Soviet Union.	1981 Ronald Reagan becomes the US President.
1990s China's economy expands rapidly.	1989 The Berlin Wall is destroyed. 1990 East and West Germany are reunited.	1990 Nelson Mandela is released.
1992 The first ever state visit to China by a Japanese emperor.	1991-4 Breakup of Yugoslavia.	1991 Gulf War to liberate Kuwait from Iraqi invasion.
1997 Hong Kong reverts from British rule to China.	1994 Channel Tunnel opened. 1999 NATO intervention in Kosovo.	1993 Bill Clinton becomes US President. 1994 Nelson Mandela elected President of South Africa.
2001 China admitted to the World Trade Organisation.	2002 Euro currency comes into use.	2000 George W. Bush becomes US President. 2001 Terrorist attacks on New York and Washington D.C.

46

Glossary

A

afterlife: many people believe that when you die you are reborn into another world. This is called the afterlife.

allies: people who are united in a cause, such as a war, by an official agreement.

archaeologist: a person who studies the past by methodically **excavating** ancient sites and artefacts.

arranged marriage: a marriage which is arranged by people other than the bridge and groom.

astronomy: the name given to the study of everything in the universe.

B

bronzes: a name for a sculpture, statue or crafted object made of bronze.

C

calligraphy: beautiful handwriting that is thought of as an art form.

cartography: the name given to the practice of making maps.

celestial globe: a model of how the universe is thought to look.

colonies: land claimed and controlled by a power outside its boundaries.

communes: groups of people who live together and share work and possessions.

D

dynasty: a series of related rulers.

E

envoy: a messenger or representative of a king or queen.

ethnic: the name given to groups of people who have things like race, religion or language in common.

eunuch: a male servant who is castrated (has part of his reproductive organs removed so that he cannot have children) employed in many of the imperial households.

excavated: something which is dug up in a methodical and scientific manner.

exported: goods transported out of a country for sale abroad are exported.

G

geologist: someone who studies the structure and history of the Earth.

grasslands: land (usually flat) where grass grows as the most common plant.

guerrilla: soldiers who do not belong to an official army. Guerrillas use different fighting tactics from national armies, usually involving ambushes and sabotage.

H

Huns: several **nomadic** tribes of Asia and eastern Europe.

I

Imperial concubine: the second or third wife of a Chinese emperor.

incentive: an extra reason to do something.

industrial: anything connected with the production of goods with technology.

inscriptions: a series of words or pictures carved or written on to a surface.

J

Jesuit: a member of the Roman Catholic Order of Jesus, founded by St. Ignatius in the sixteenth century. The Jesuits worked all over the world as **missionaries**.

K

Karl Marx: (1818-83) a German writer who founded the political theory of Communism.

M

Manchu: an **ethnic** people who live in north-east China.

meditate: to think about something.

Mesopotamia: the area between the Euphrates and Tigris rivers (modern-day Iraq). The civilizations of Sumer and Babylon thrived in Mesopotamia.

millet: a grass that is grown for grain and to feed animals.

missionaries: people who try to convert people from one religion to another.

mountain sickness: an illness caused by lack of oxygen which involves bad headaches, shortness of breath and sickness.

Muslims: people who follow the religion of Islam founded by the Prophet Mohammed in Arabia in 622CE. Muslims try to live their lives according to the teachings of the Quran which they believe to be the words of God as heard by Mohammed.

N

Nationalist: beliefs held by people within a country which are based on that country's identity.

Neolithic: the period of history from 9000-6000 BCE in south-west Asia and 4000-2400 BCE in Europe. Neolithic people used stone tools to farm the land.

nomads: people who travel from place to place.

O

officials: people who have jobs in government.

opium: an addictive drug made by drying the juice of poppy seeds.

P

pagodas: beautifully-decorated temples or towers, usually many storeys high.

Persian: anything relating to the country of Persia. Persia changed its name to Iran in 1935.

physics: the study of energy and matter.

polo: a team game played on horseback.

pomegranates: the fruit of the pomegranate tree which usually grows in **semi-tropical** areas of the world. Pomegranates are about the size of oranges and contain many red seeds.

porcelain: a fine hard ceramic mixture (fired clay) that is white in colour.

Privy Council: the name of the group of officials who govern the country at the instruction of the emperor.

R

rationing: a ration is a set or restricted amount of something (usually food).

Red Guards: army-like units of young people who were taught to destroy anything connected with history during the Cultural Revolution.

S

saltpetre: one of the explosive ingredients of gunpowder.

Sanskrit: the ancient language of India.

scholar: a learned or well-educated person.

seals: stamps with personal names or official titles on them.

semi-tropical: places near, but not in, the tropics.

sulphur: a light-yellow powder that smells terrible and has many different uses in medicine and industry.

T

terracotta: unfired (or unbaked) clay.

textiles: material woven from spun threads.

treasury: the name for the government or emperor's store of money, gold or treasures.

Turks: people from Turkey (in southern Europe, next to Greece).

Z

zoologist: someone who studies animals.

Index

Numbers in **bold** indicate an illustration. Words in **bold** are in the glossary on page 47.

This edition published in 2003 by
Belitha Press
A member of **Chrysalis** Books plc
64 Brewery Road, London N7 9NT

ISBN 1 84138 651 0

Typeset by Chambers Wallace, London

Printed in Hong Kong

British Library Cataloguing in Publication Data for this book is available from the British Library.

Editor: Jill A. Laidlaw
Designer: Andrew Oliver
Picture researcher: Anne-Marie Ehrlich
Map overlays: Hard Lines
Consultant: Frances Wood

Photographic credits

British Library 2, 11 below, 12 above right, 13 above right, 19 below, 21, 24 below, 25, 26 below, 30, 34. Bridgeman Art Library 35 below, 36, 37 below. British Museum 14, 20 below. Comstock 12-13. E.T. Archive 8 below, 10, 11, 15 below, 17 below, 19 above, 22 below, 23 above right, 24 above, 26 above, 28, 32-3, 35 above, 38 above left, 40 above left. Mary Evans Picture Library 39 above right. Werner Forman Archive 9, 17 above, 38 below. Sally and Richard Greenhill 7 above right. Sonia Halliday Photographs 23 centre. Robert Harding Picture Library 3, 5, 8 above, 12 below left, 27 inset, 29. Hulton-Deutsch 37 above, 40 below, 41 below. Hutchison Library titlepage, 16 above, 23 below, 27 below, 42 above, 43, 44. Institute of Verterbrate Palaeontology Beijing 7 below. Popperfoto 39 below, 40 centre inset, 41 above, 42 below. Courtesy of Brian Power 38 centre, 39 above left. Museum of Far Eastern Antiquities Stockholm 7 above. Wang Tao 33 top right, centre, bottom. Fujita Art Museum Osaka 21-2.